Beginner Guitar Lessons
Book 1

with Online Video Access

by
Peter Vogl

To access Online Video for this course, go to the following internet address:

cvls.com/extras/bgb1

Introduction

Beginner Guitar Lessons Book 1 with Online Video Access by Peter Vogl is a collection of nine video lessons for the absolute beginning guitarist. You will learn about holding the guitar and pick, playing notes and melodies, beginner chords, strumming, and more. These lessons are designed for someone who has never played guitar before and will teach them all of the necessary fundamentals for becoming a guitarist. This package contains over three hours worth of online HD video instruction. Learn how to play guitar today!

The Author

Peter started playing guitar in 2nd grade and very quickly realized his calling. He played in several bands through his years at Okemos High, and proceeded to study classical guitar in college at the University of Georgia under the tutelage of John Sutherland. After receiving his undergraduate degree in Classical Guitar Performance Peter continued with his studies on a assistantship at James Madison University. While there he taught classes as large as 110 people at both James Madison and Mary Baldwin College.

Peter moved back to Georgia and began playing the club circuit in Atlanta as a soloist and with a multitude of bands. He also founded and managed several schools of guitar including the Guitar Learning Center. During this time Peter produced many products for Watch & Learn Inc. such as *The Guitarist's Chord Book, The Guitarist's Scale Book, Intro to Blues Guitar, Intro to Rock Guitar, The Guitarist's Tablature Book, & The Let's Jam! Series.*

In the 90's Peter met Jan Smith and began to play with the Jan Smith Band performing on several of her CDs including Nonstop Thrill, Surrender, and Resurrection. In 2001 Peter moved into Jan Smith Studios where he continues to teach and do session work with local and national talent.

Peter has performed on stage with talents such as Michael Bolton, Cee-Lo, Kelly Price, Steve Vai, Earl Klugh, Sharon Isbon, and Sleepy Brown. In collaboration with the NARAS organization he is the band leader each year at the Heroes Award Dinner in Atlanta.

Watch & Learn Products Really Work

35 years ago, Watch & Learn, Inc. revolutionized music instructional courses by developing well thought out, step-by-step instructional methods that were tested for effectiveness on beginners before publication. These products, which have dramatically improved the understanding and success of beginning students, have evolved into the Watch & Learn system that continues to set the standard of music instruction today. This has resulted in sales of more than three million products since 1979.

More Books by Peter Vogl

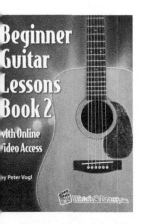

Beginner Guitar Lessons Book 2 with Online Video Access is the follow-up to this course. Learn the tips and tricks that separate a real guitarist from a beginner. Peter will teach you techniques like hammer-ons, pull-offs, and slides along with new chords, progressions, and strumming patterns. Finally, you'll learn how to make basic progressions more exciting by adding embellishments and mixing in riffs with the chords. Using all of the concepts taught in these lessons, you'll be ready to start creating your own music. This course includes over three hours of online HD video instruction.

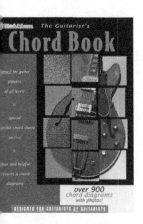

The Guitarist's Chord Book by Peter Vogl is a 144 page book that contains over 900 chords with photos to clearly illustrate each chord and each note of the chord is labeled. It also contains a special moveable chords section with the most widely used shapes for each class of chord. Peter Vogl has also included goodies from his bag of tricks to give you new sounds, shapes, and inspirations for song arrangements. The chord shapes have been reviewed by guitar teachers and players across the country. This is a must read for guitar players of all levels.

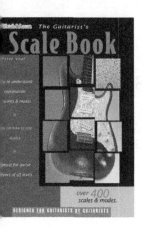

The Guitarist's Scale Book by Peter Vogl is a complete scale encyclopedia for guitar with over 400 scales and modes. It contains scale diagrams with notation and tablature for each scale and tips on how and when to use each scale. This scale book also contains outside jazz scales, exotic scales, Peter's own Cross-Stringing scales, and easy to understand explanations of scales and modes. This is the only guitar scale book you'll ever need.

These products are available on Amazon.com. If you have any questions, problems, or comments, please contact us at:

Watch & Learn, Inc.
2947 East Point St.
East Point, GA 30344
800-416-7088
sales@cvls.com

Table of Contents

1. Basics & Beginner Chords

The Guitar

The sound hole on an acoustic guitar is where the sound of the strings becomes louder. On an electric guitar, the pickups are used to collect the sound and make it louder.

The pick guard does exactly what its name says it does. It protects the wood on your guitar from being damaged by the pick while you play.

The bridge holds the strings in place just like the nut does at the other end of the neck.

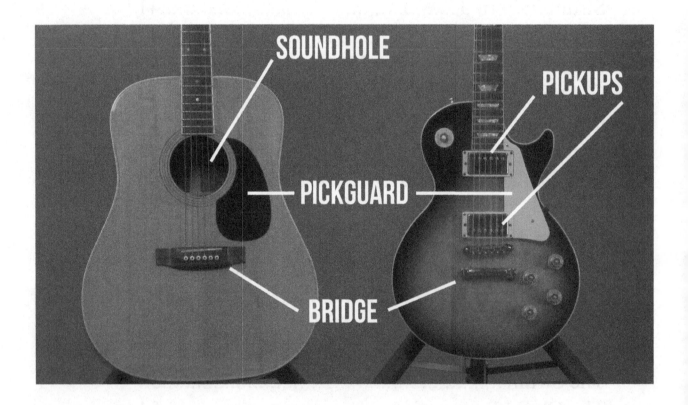

To access Online Video for this course, go to the following internet address:

cvls.com/extras/bgb1

The Tuners, Headstock, Nut, and Frets

The tuners are important for keeping your guitar in tune and for restringing the guitar. The nut is where the strings first contact the guitar and the grooves in the nut allow the strings to slide through. The frets are where the strings rest when you press down a string in a fret space. As you go up the neck towards the body, the pitches get higher on each string.

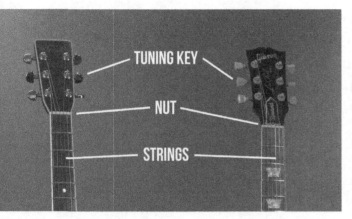 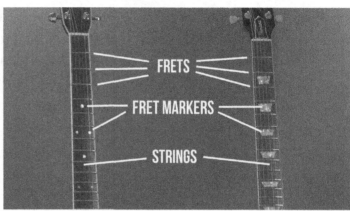

The Strings

The strings on the guitar are numbered from the bottom up or the smallest string to the highest string - 1,2,3,4,5,6. They each have a letter name or a note that they are tuned to. Starting with the first string, they are E,B,G,D,A,E. This will become very important to memorize as this course progresses.

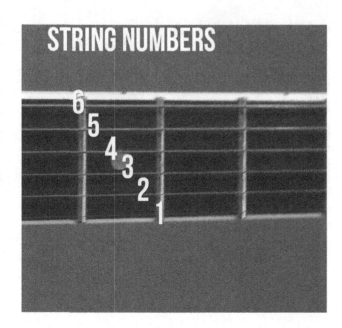 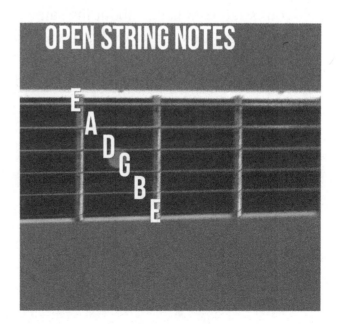

Sitting Position

For a right handed person, the guitar should be sitting on the right leg slightly leaning against the torso. The right elbow should be resting on the upper right hand corner of the guitar with the arm able to move freely. Your left arm should be able to hang from the shoulder with the thumb placed on the back of the guitar. It is usually best to place both feet squarely on the floor. Avoid slumping or rounding the back while playing, as this can cause back damage and pain over time.

Standing Position

The guitar should hang at about the same spot on your body as if you were sitting down. Look at the height of your guitar when you are sitting and adjust your strap so it hangs about the same height against your torso. It's always a good idea to keep a hand on the guitar when you are standing and using a strap. To keep the guitar even more secure, you may want to use a strap lock.

Tuning the Guitar

The most common way to tune your guitar is with either an electronic tuner or a tuning app. Luckily, most of these work the same way. If you play the 3rd string (G), you may see a G show up on the screen. If the note your string is playing is too low or flat, you might see an F or F$\sharp$. You will need to tighten your string a little until you see the G show up in the middle. If the note played by your 3rd string is too high, you may see A$\flat$ or A. This means you need to loosen your string a little.

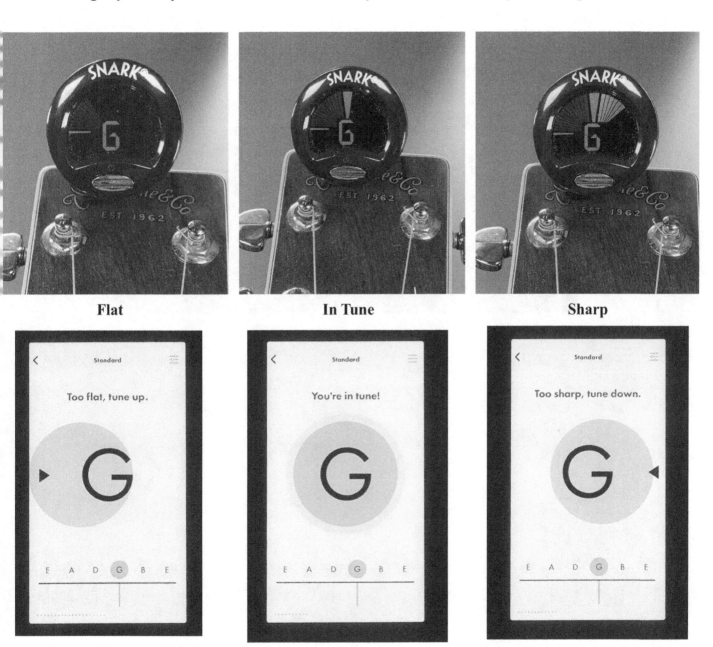

| Flat | In Tune | Sharp |

We then need to repeat this process for all six strings (E, A, D, G, B, E) until they are playing the correct note. It's important that you tune your guitar at the start of each practice session. Playing an out of tune guitar is like baking a cake with the wrong ingredients. No matter how hard you try, it won't end up tasting very good. Even famous guitarists would sound bad if they play out of tune guitars.

Thumb Position

The left thumb pad should be placed on the back of the guitar neck. This position will vary according to what your hand size is, what the size of the guitar neck is, and what technique you are doing, but our "core" position will be about 50 to 75 percent up the back of the neck. The thumb pressure is generally light and able to move all directions on the neck. Pressure on the thumb increases depending on the technique. Barre chords, for example, will require much more pressure.

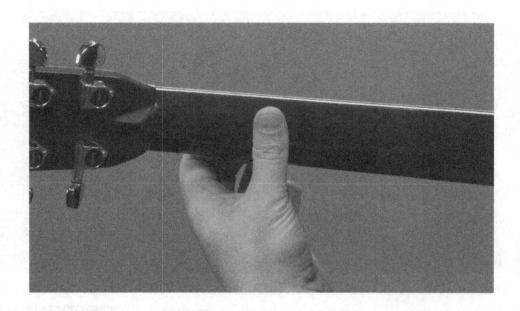

The Guitar Neck and the Left Hand

The metal bars on the neck of the guitar are called frets. When pressing down a string, the string rests on the crown of the fret. This is where the note is really being sounded from.

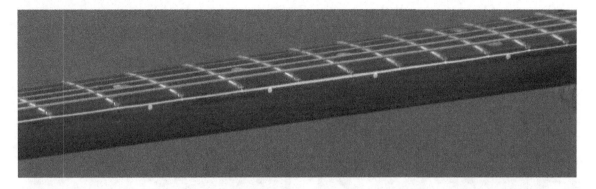

You want to press down a string only as hard as it takes to get a clean note. Pressing too hard can cause many issues. In order to do this, you should place your finger toward the front of the fret as this is the place that requires the least amount of pressure to get a clean note. Remember, we are not pressing down the string to the wood of the guitar neck, only down to the crown of the fret, which is higher than the wood.

Correct

Too far from fret

11

Exercise 1 - Em Chord

Use your 1st finger to press down the 5th string 2nd fret and your 2nd finger to press down the 4th string 2nd fret. Keep your thumb somewhat low on the back of the neck and play on the tips of your fingers. Try not to touch any other strings with your fingers. Then strum all the strings. This chord is called E minor.

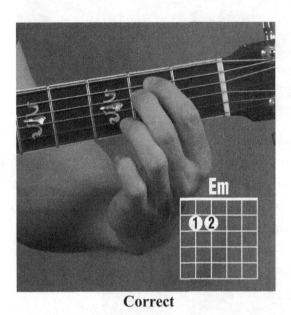

Correct

Too far from fret

Chord Diagrams

The chord diagram represents an E minor chord labeled Em. This little "m" stands for minor. The top thick horizontal line is the nut of the guitar neck. The horizontal lines below that are the frets. The vertical lines are the strings on the guitar with the 6th string to the left and the first string to the right. The two dots tell us where to place fingers on the guitar. They are both in the 2nd fret with the 1st finger on the 5th string and the 2nd finger on the 4th string.

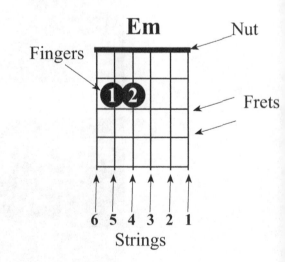

12

Exercise 2 - Am Chord

The Am chord has the 1st finger on the 2nd string 1st fret, the 2nd finger on the 4th string 2nd fret and the 3rd finger on the 3rd string 2nd fret. Play towards the front of the frets and keep your thumb on the back of neck low. Strum from the 5th string down.

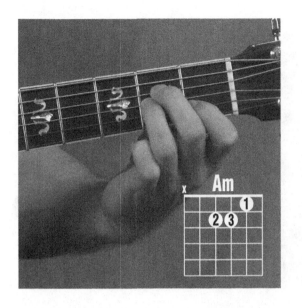

Exercise 3 - D⁷ Chord

The D^7 chord is played with the 1st finger on the 2nd string 1st fret, the 2nd finger on the 3rd string 2nd fret, and the 3rd finger on the 1st string 2nd fret. Strum from the 4th string down. Be careful not to mute the 2nd string by letting your 2nd finger lay across it.

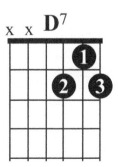

13

Exercise 4 - G Major Chord

To make the G chord, place your 2nd finger on the 6th string 3rd fret, the 1st finger on the 5th string 2nd fret, and the 3rd finger on the 1st string 3d fret. Strum all the strings. Remember to keep your thumb low on the back of the neck.

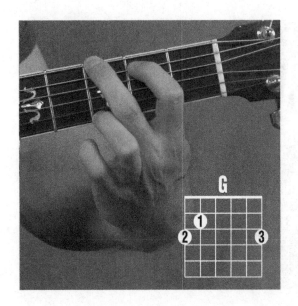

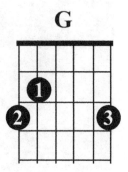

The Pivot Finger

When changing chords, there are two extremely important techniques we will learn. One is the pivot finger and the other is the guide finger. The *pivot finger* is a finger that stays still while changing chords. It is a very important technique to enable smooth chord changes.

Exercise 5

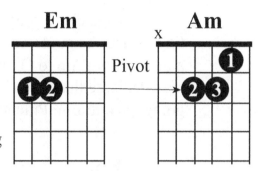

Practice changing chords from Em to Am. Notice the 2nd finger on the 4th string can stay in place while changing. This is called a *pivot finger*. Whenever you can leave a finger in place from one chord to the next, it will cut down on mistakes and allow an extra note to ring through the chord change creating a smoother sound. In this case, leave the 2nd finger in place while changing from Em to Am. Whenever possible, use pivot fingers.

The Guide Finger

A *guide finger* is a finger that stays on the same string but has to slide to its next position.

Exercise 6

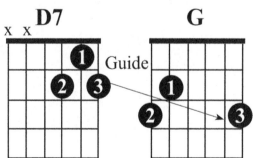

When changing from D^7 to G the, 3rd finger can stay on the same string but must slide from the 2nd fret to the 3rd fret. This is called a guide finger. This is generally a multi-step process. First, lift the other fingers in the D^7 chord (1st and 2nd) leaving the 3rd finger where it is. Then slide the 3rd finger up to the 3rd fret and finally, place the other fingers down for the G chord. Practice this chord change and technique. Whenever possible, use a guide finger. Practice changing from D^7 to G.

A Chord Progression in G

Now that we have learned how to change chords using pivot and guide fingers, let's use these techniques to play a chord progression. A chord progression is a series of chords played one after the other.

Exercise 7

Here is a chord progression in the key of G. Pay attention to all of the pivot fingers and the guide finger at the end. Changing from Em to Am, the 2nd finger is a pivot. From Am to D^7, the 1st finger is a pivot, and from D^7 to G the 3rd finger is a guide. Note that when starting the progression over again, the 1st finger is a pivot going back to Em. Practice this chord progression.

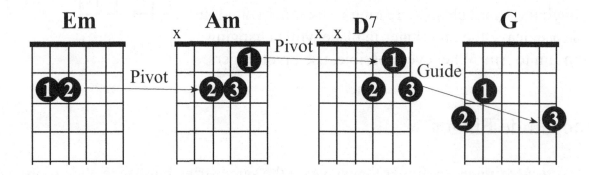

The Pick

I recommend most beginners start with a medium pick gauge pick and use the most common size. Nothing too big or small and steer away from odd shapes. As you progress, you can determine if you want to go with a heavier pick or what shape you like the best. Picks are made of different materials so they all have a slightly different tone. You will probably find a favorite pick after trying a few.

Holding The Pick

When holding the pick, place the wide part of the pick between the pad of your thumb and your index finger's first joint. This should leave you plenty of pick to play with. The other fingers are curled in towards the palm of the hand and not extended outward. The index finger is also slightly curled in, so the tip of the finger is not pointed in the same direction as the tip of the pick.

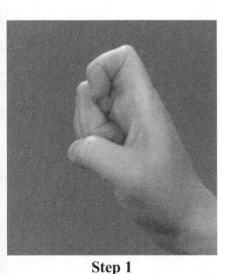
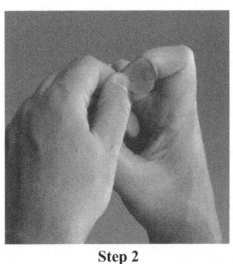
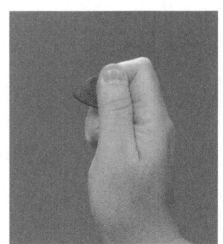

Step 1 **Step 2** **Step 3**

Reading Tablature or Tab

Much of guitar music is written using tablature. It is a method much easier to read than standard music notation. We will be using tablature throughout this course, so it is important that you learn how to read it.

The six lines of tablature represent the 6 strings of the guitar. The lowest line is the lowest string on the guitar or number 6 (the lowest in pitch and thickest string). The numbers on the strings represent the frets to be played. In the example below, the first number, reading left to right, is a zero on the 6th string. This means play an open 6th string with no fingers on it (only the 6th string and no others). It is written twice so you play it two times in a row. The next number is a 4 on the 6th string, so play the 4th fret 6th string. The next number is a 2 written on the 5th string, so play the 2nd fret 5th string. After that, we have four numbers on the 4th string. They are 0, 4, 2, 0. Play those frets in that order. The numbers above the tablature staff are the fingers to use. Played all together, this is a guitar riff or melody. Tablature is extremely good at writing out these sort of things. Since it is so widely used, be sure to get used to reading it.

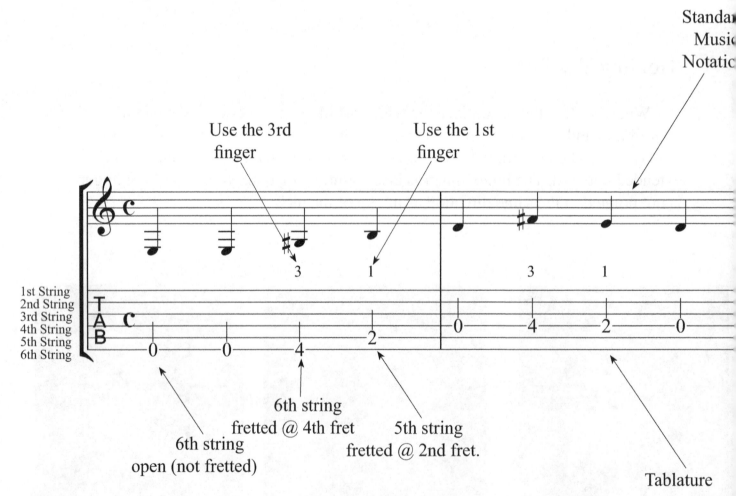

18

2. Strumming & More Chords

The guitar is a percussion instrument, so playing rhythm is the most important thing we do. Strumming is a large part of this. The core technique we will learn to use when strumming is *constant motion*.

Constant Motion

The technique of constant motion means when strumming, our strumming hand will be constantly moving up and down, whether we are hitting the strings or not. The motion starts from the elbow down through the forearm with some wrist rotation as well. The forearm and wrist should stay relaxed. The range of motion is generally from the top of the sound hole to the bottom. Sometimes it will be longer or shorter depending on what we are trying to do. Think of brushing the strings rather than striking them.

Muted Strumming

One of the best ways to practice strumming is the muted strumming drill. This takes our playing into the bare bones of being a percussionist and allows us to focus solely on the strumming hand. Lay the left hand across the strings, lightly touching them in order to mute the notes. Be sure to not press too hard with your left hand or you will play notes. We want only muted tones, no pitches.

Muted Strumming

Exercise 8

In this exercise, use muted strumming to play the rhythm. It is important to stay in motion with the right hand even when you are not playing anything on beats 2, 3, and 4. Continue the strumming motion with the right hand hovering over the strings but not actually playing them. Strum on beat 1 using a downstroke. This constant motion of our right hand will be our core strumming technique.

Exercise 9

In this example of muted strumming, play on beats 1 and 3 with a downstroke. Stay in motion with your right hand during the other beats using constant motion. Keep you forearm and wrist moving together in a fluid relaxed fashion.

Exercise 10

In this exercise, we add eighth notes which are twice as fast as quarter notes. Count 1 2 3 and 4. We will play on beat 1 and 3 and on the and or upstroke of beat 3. Stay in motion throughout this exercise.

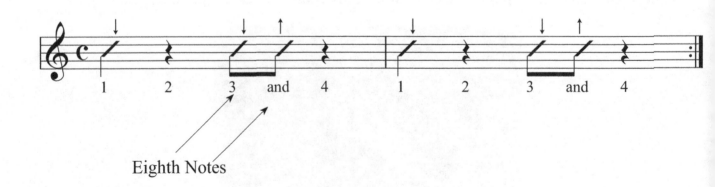

Eighth Notes

Strumming with Chords

Now let's add a musical component to our strumming and try out our patterns with chords.

Exercise 11

In this exercise, we'll use the strum pattern from Exercise 10 over an Em chord. Remember to stay in motion.

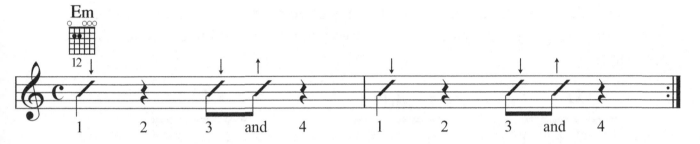

Exercise 12

Now try this strumming pattern with an Em chord. Play on beat 1, play twice on beat 2, and then play on beats 3 and 4. Beat 2 is a down and upstroke. Stay in motion with the strumming hand and remember to feel like you are brushing the strings.

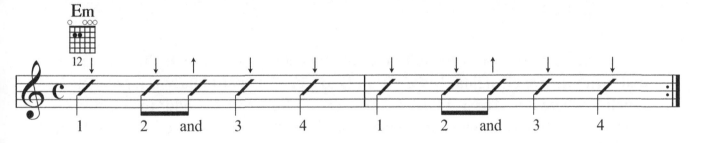

To access Online Video for this course, go to the following internet address:

cvls.com/extras/bgb1

More Chord Progressions

Since we now have several strum patterns to practice, let's turn our attention to some new chords and chord progressions.

D Cadd⁹ G

Start by learning these three chords. When strumming the D major chord, strum from the 4th string down. When playing Cadd^9, strum from the 5th string down. With G major, strum all the strings (this is the four finger G chord). Play towards the front of the frets and on the tips of your fingers. Be careful to touch only the string you are trying to press down and not let you fingers mute other strings.

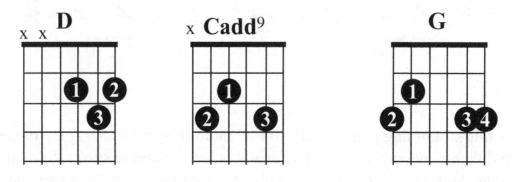

Exercise 13

In this exercise, we will work on changing chords. Strum each chord once and then practice changing. Notice from D to Cadd^9, the 3rd finger is a pivot and remains where it is. The 3rd finger is also a pivot finger from Cadd^9 to G. From G, we have to return to D again and once more the 3rd finger is a pivot. The 3rd finger should never have to move during this progression. Practice until these become comfortable.

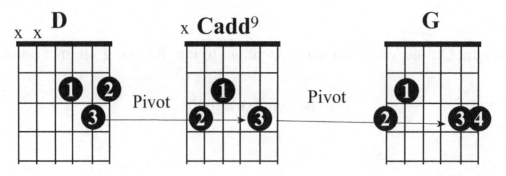

E A^6/^{9} EM^7

Here is another chord progression, this time in the key of E. These chords will sound beautiful when played correctly. Notice the 4 on the left side of the EM^7 chord diagram. This indicates that we've moved up to the 4th fret with our 1st finger. Your 3rd and 4th fingers are now on the 6th fret. We've effectively moved the A^6/^{9} chord two frets up the neck.

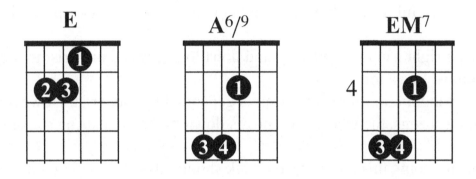

Exercise 14

Practice the chord changes for this new chord progression. We will be moving up and down the neck a bit here. The 1st finger is a guide finger throughout. Remember, a guide finger stays on the same string but slides to the next position. Keep your thumb low on the back of the neck to facilitate the stretches and play towards the front of the frets.

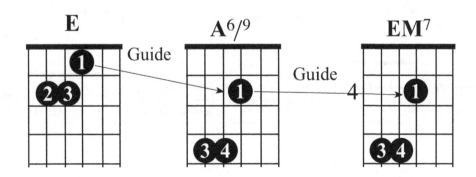

23

3. Scales & Alternate Picking

Let's change it up a little here and work on a new right hand technique that will prove useful when playing scales or melodies.

Alternate Picking

It's going to be important to focus on a few right hand positioning and movement keys in order to execute this technique correctly. Watching the video will prove very useful for this but here are a few of the things to keep in mind.

1. Let your right hand move freely and don't lock down your wrist to the guitar. It's almost like a mini strum.
2. The picking motion for each string is generated by the wrist. However, when changing strings, the whole arm moves down to the next string starting at the elbow.
3. If you are doing this correctly, the pick should play each string with the same angle and not change as you move down through the strings.

Exercise 15

In this exercise, we will play only open strings, so your left hand won't be doing anything. Pick each open string two times using alternate picking (Down, Up, Down, Up) then move on to the next string. Keep the alternation going at all times. The arrows above the notes show you the pick direction.

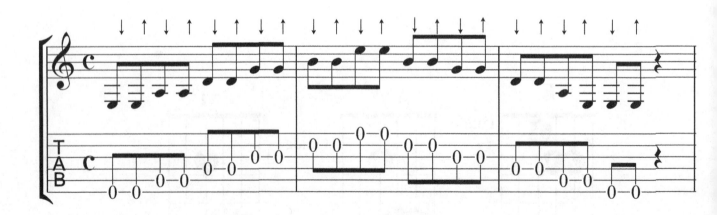

Exercise 16

Here is a slight variation on the last exercise. This time play three times on each string. Since this is an odd number, each string should start with an opposite motion. The 6th string should start with an downstroke, 5th string with a upstroke, and so on.

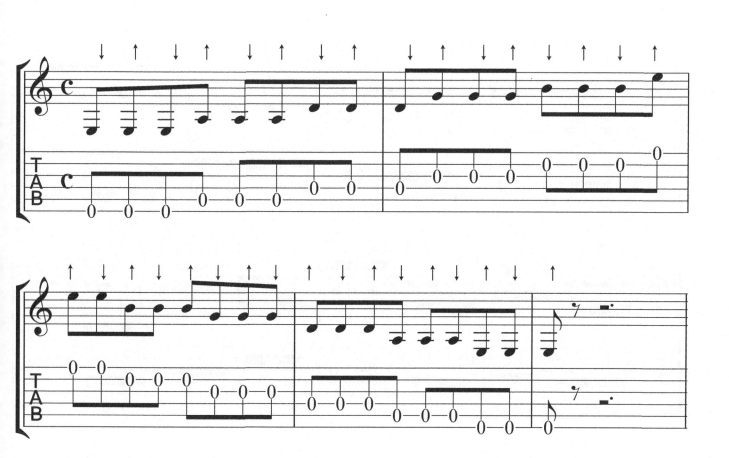

To access Online Video for this course, go to the following internet address:

cvls.com/extras/bgb1

Exercise 17

Here is one more variation of the same exercise. This time play four times on each string.

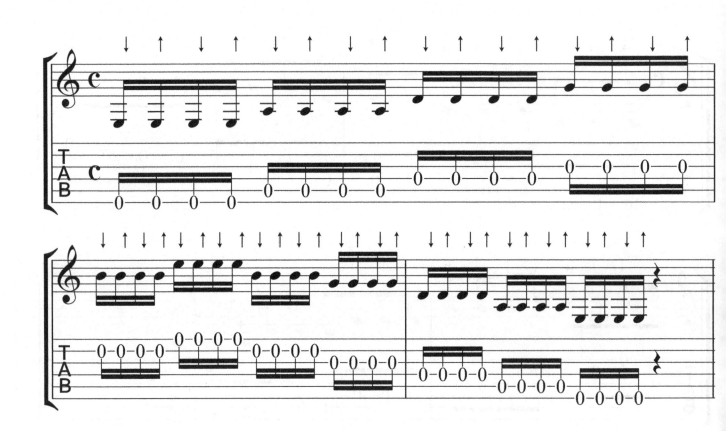

First Position Scales

The Em Pentatonic Scale

The Em pentatonic scale is one of the most widely used scales on guitar for creating melodies and connecting chords together. This scale is a must for all guitar players.

Exercise 18

Practice the Em pentatonic scale below. When first learning this scale, don't worry too much about alternate picking. Once you are able to play the scale, make sure to apply the alternate picking technique. Keep your left thumb low on the back of the neck and play towards the front of the frets. We will use the device "frets and fingers the same" which means whatever fret you are in, that is the finger you will use (1st fret 1st finger, 2nd fret 2nd finger, and so on). Practice slowly at first, then build up speed as you get more comfortable with the scale.

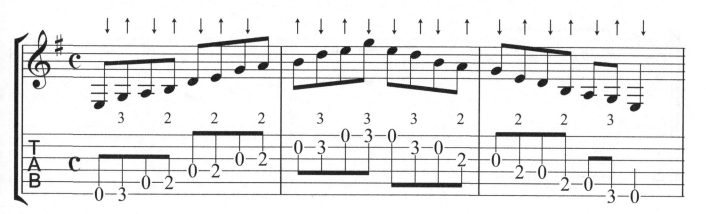

The E Blues Scale

This next scale is very similar to the Em pentatonic scale with one extra note added.

Exercise 19

Practice the E blues scale using alternate picking. Be sure to keep the alternation going when you change strings. Pay particular attention when you are playing the scale backwards as beginners tend to repeat upstrokes on the way back.

The G Major Scale

The major scale is perhaps the most widely known scale. Here it is in G major.

Exercise 20

Practice the G major scale forwards and backwards. The alternate picking technique becomes a little more complicated with this scale. Keep your thumb low on the back of the neck.

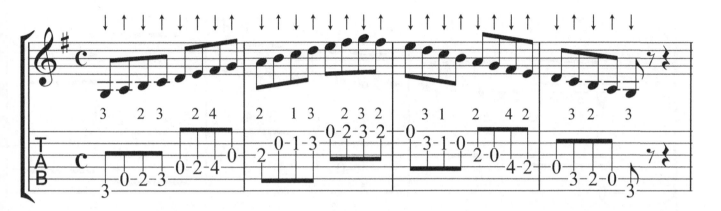

The A Minor Scale

The minor scale is also an extremely important scale. A good one to learn first is the A minor scale.

Exercise 21

Practice the A minor scale using all of the techniques we have been practicing so far. Remember to makes scales a regular part of your guitar practice.

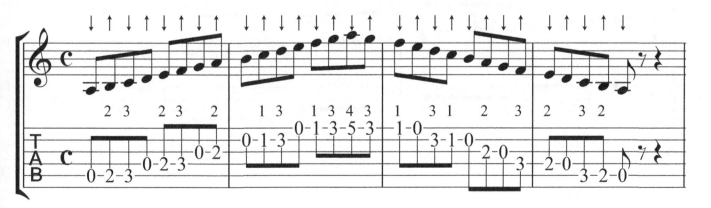

The Chromatic Scale

Chromatic means moving by half steps or by one fret at a time. This scale may be easy to remember, but it is a challenge to play smoothly.

Exercise 22

Practice the chromatic scale slowly at first and be conscious of good hand position. Pay attention to the fingerings and try to keep the fingers floating above the frets.

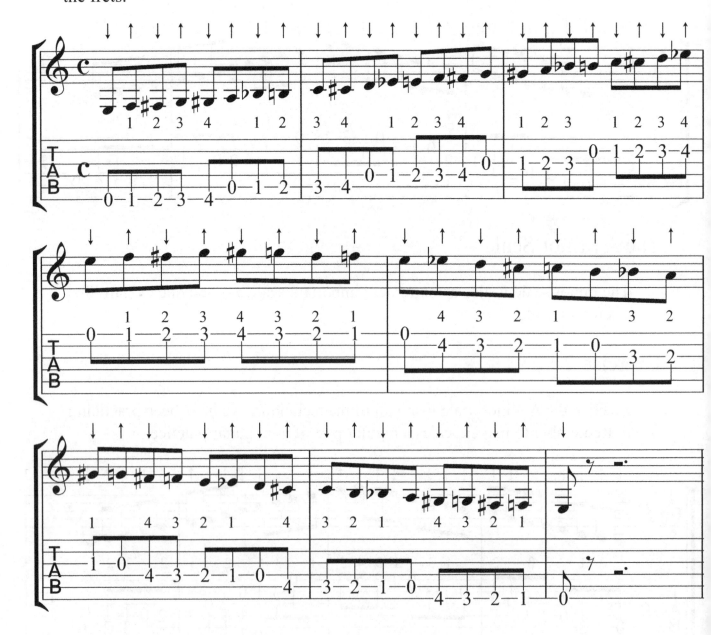

4. New Chords & Strumming Tips

In this next section, we add more chords to our chord vocabulary and a few new strum patterns. The A minor chord we have learned before, but new chords will be Am^7, FM^7, and E^7.

Exercise 23

Begin by practicing each one of these chords on their own. Make sure you keep the thumb on the back of neck low. Play on the tips of your fingers and towards the front of the frets. Try to play each string of the chord clearly without buzzing or muted notes.

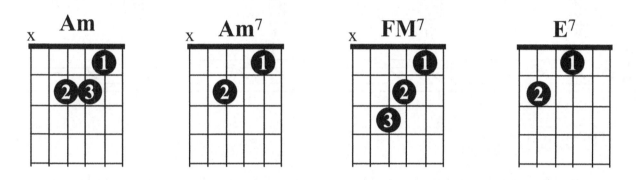

Exercise 24

When you can make each chord clearly, then work on changing chords. Between Am and Am^7, you can leave fingers 1 and 2 in place (pivot fingers) and simply lift the 3rd finger. Make sure the open 3rd string isn't muted. From Am^7 to FM^7, leave the 1st finger still. From FM^7 to E^7, you will need to lift everything since there is no pivot or guide finger. Practice these chord changes.

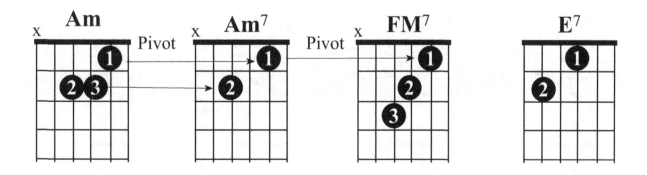

Am, Am⁷, FM⁷, E⁷ with Strum Pattern

Now that we have these chords down, let's add a strumming pattern.

Exercise 25

While playing this chord progression, we will use a new strum pattern. The pattern has two downstrokes to start it off and then a stop or mute with your right hand. To execute the mute, bring your right hand to the strings and mute all of them. It is a rhythmic stop, and by that, I mean it happens directly on beat three and we should hear nothing on beats three and four. Think of it as down, down, stop.

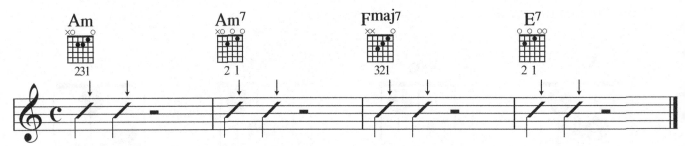

Arpeggios

An arpeggio is playing one note of a chord at a time. Let's try this technique with the previous chord progression.

Exercise 26

In this exercise, we will play one note at a time of each chord. Pay close attention to the tablature and the strings you are playing from each chord. Also pay attention to the pick directions. When going from the lowest note to the highest, use a downstroke. When going from highest note to lowest, use an upstroke.

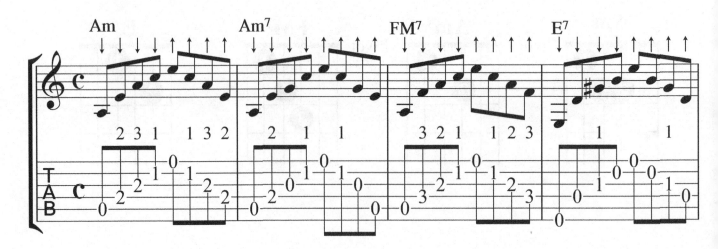

5. Simple Melodies

Since we have expanded our chord and strumming vocabulary in the last section, let's now focus on playing some melodies on the guitar. Melodies are similar to scales, but are more musically interesting. These melodies will help our technique develop.

Exercise 27

Here is a melody starting on the 5th string. Pay attention to the fingerings and make sure to use alternate picking.

Exercise 28

This melody is very similar to the previous one. We simply start this one on the 5th string. Practice both until they are easy to play.

Exercise 29

This next melody starts on the 6th string. The first note lasts for a beat and a half, so pay attention to the rhythm.

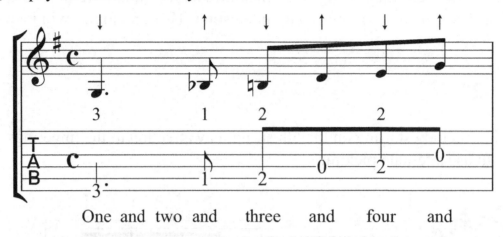

One and two and three and four and

Exercise 30

This melody is the same as the previous one except it is down a string, starting on the 5th string. The last note is played on the 1st fret 2nd string rather than an open string.

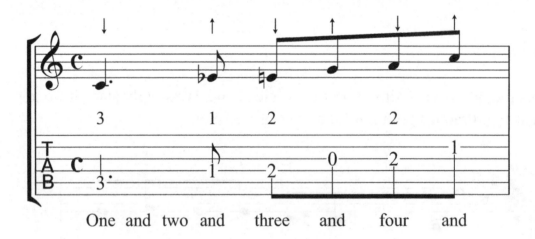

One and two and three and four and

Exercise 31

In this exercise, we will play a melody that starts at the 5th fret on the 1st string using our pinky. Remember to use alternate picking.

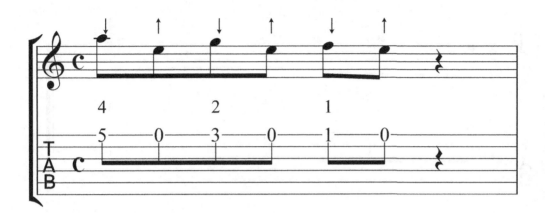

Exercise 32

This exercise is chromatic or moving by half steps. That means it moves one fret at a time on the guitar. This is a great exercise to work on developing good hand position. Pay attention to the fingerings, keep your thumb low on the back of the neck, and use alternate picking.

Exercise 33

This exercise is the same as the previous one, only this time we'll start on the first string. It's a slightly different hand position and again a great exercise for the left hand.

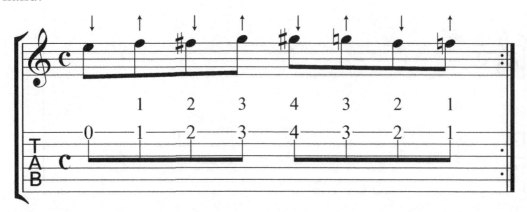

Exercise 34

In this melody, we will play more than one string at a time to create harmonies. This is a stock guitar riff and is a fantastic one to know. Use only downstrokes when playing this melody and make sure your finger only touches one string at a time with your left hand.

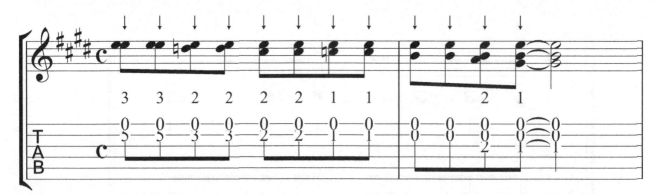

Exercise 35

Here is an exercise to help you develop your alternate picking speed. This will enable you to play faster rhythms when needed. Practice slowly at first, keeping motions small and relaxed. Then, gradually build up speed.

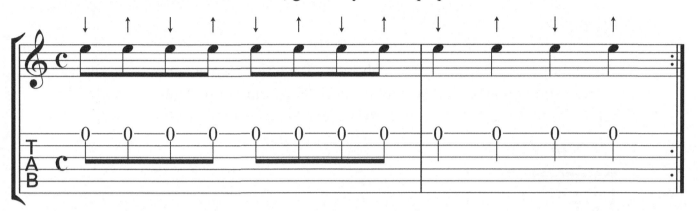

Exercise 36

This melody is what is called a sequence and it uses the Em pentatonic scale. Each bar can be considered a drill itself. Playing this will not only help your melodic playing but make you more comfortable with the Em pentatonic scale. Practice slowly at first and try practicing each measure one at a time.

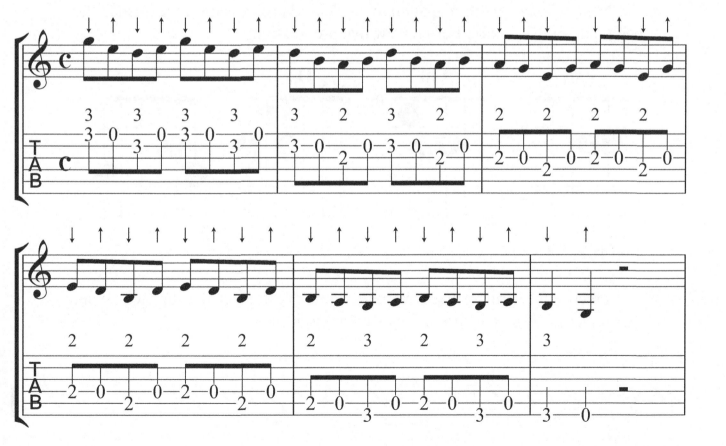

6. More Strum Patterns

In this section, we will work on common strum patterns and play them with chords. Lets start by using an Em chord. Here is our first strum pattern.

Exercise 37

During this exercise, use an Em chord and practice a basic strum pattern. Keep your strum short and stay in constant motion. Make sure your right arm and wrist are relaxed, allowing them to rotate. You should see the pick rotating as well.

Strum Patterns with Chord Progressions

Next, let's try this strum pattern over a chord progression we learned at the beginning of this course. Let's review that progression:

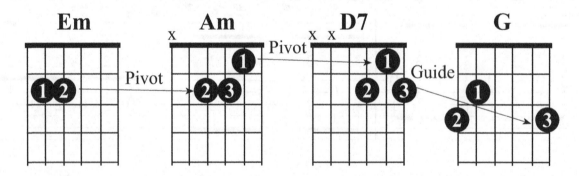

Exercise 38

Practice this strum pattern over the chords. Next, try it at a slow tempo and remember to keep your strumming hand in motion.

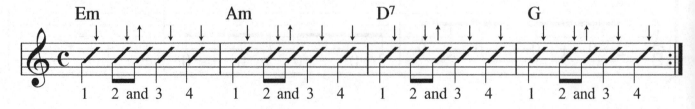

Strum Pattern 2

The next pattern we will try while playing a D chord.

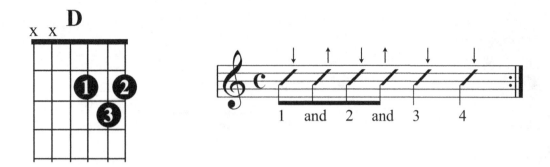

Here is another chord progression we learned earlier in the course. Review it before playing the next exercise.

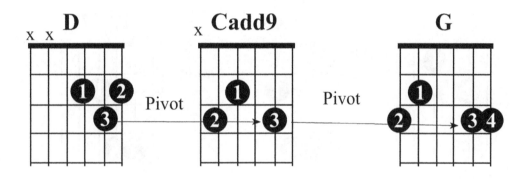

Exercise 39

Now try playing our second strum pattern over these chords. Do good clean chord changes and keep your strumming hand in constant motion.

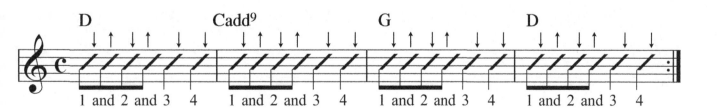

Strum Pattern 3

Try the next strum pattern while playing an E major chord.

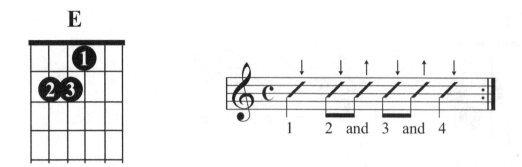

Here's another chord progression from earlier in this course. Review the chords and the changes. Once they are smooth, try going on to the next exercise.

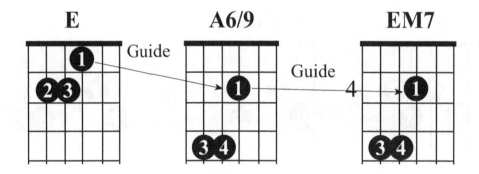

Exercise 40

Try strum pattern three while playing these chords. Take your time and don't try to play too fast. The goal is to be able to keep the pattern going and change chords without any breaks or faltering. This could take a fair amount of time and practice so don't get discouraged. Consistent practice will get you there.

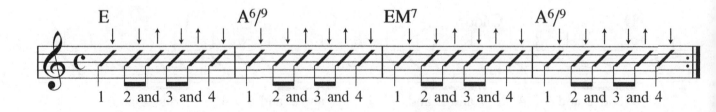

Strum Pattern 4

Let's work on the next pattern while playing an Am chord.

One more chord progression from earlier in this course. Practice the chords and the changes.

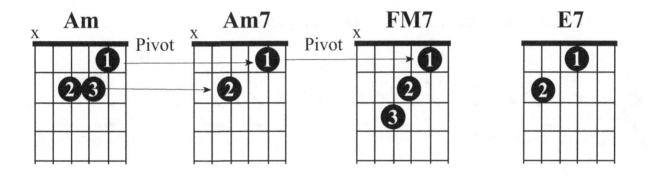

Exercise 41

Now try playing strum pattern 4 and this chord progression. Make sure you stay in motion with your right hand. Try to make the chord changes in time.

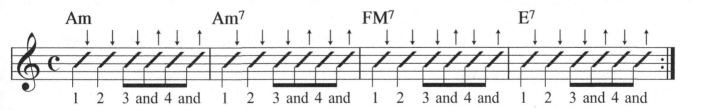

Using All 4 Strum Patterns

In the next series of exercises, try all four patterns over our first chord progression: Em, Am, D⁷, G.

Exercise 42

Since we have already played strum pattern 1 over this progression, try strum pattern 2.

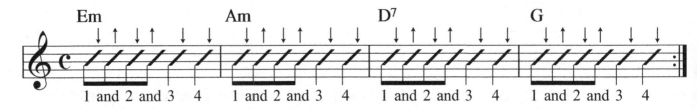

Exercise 43

Here is strum pattern 3 over the same progression.

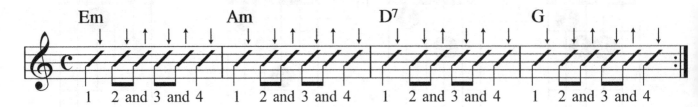

Exercise 44

Now try strum pattern 4 over this same progression.

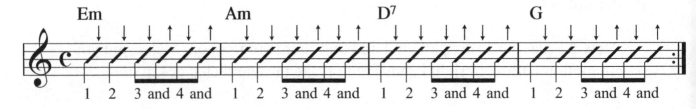

Exercise 45

Try switching the strum pattern each bar as you play through the progression.

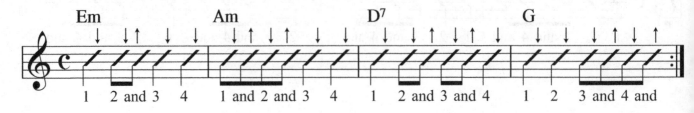

7. The Most Common Strum Pattern

In this section, we will cover the most common strum pattern played on guitar. First, let's work on a new chord progression to use with this pattern.

Exercise 46

Start by working on each chord. The G major chord below is the 4 finger G chord. The second chord is called D with an F sharp in the bass. The first letter of the name is the chord and the letter after the forward slash is a specific bass or low note of the chord. So this is a D major chord with a specific bass note. Em and Am^7 we have learned before. The last chord is D^7 with an F sharp in the bass. This means it is a D7 chord with a specific bass note. Practice these chords and then we will work on how to move from one chord to the other.

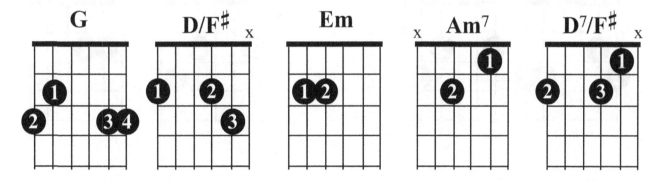

Changing Chords

Now let's work on changing chords cleanly and smoothly during this progression. To move from G to D/F♯, the 3rd finger is a pivot so keep it still. From D/F♯ to Em, we don't have a pivot or guide, so just bring your 1st and 2nd finger together to the 5th and 4th strings. From Em to Am^7, your 2nd finger is a pivot. From Am^7 to D^7/F♯, the 1st finger is a pivot. To complete the progression, go back to the first chord. From D^7/F♯ to G, the 2nd finger is a guide finger on the 6th string. Slide it from the 2nd fret to the 3rd and complete the chord.

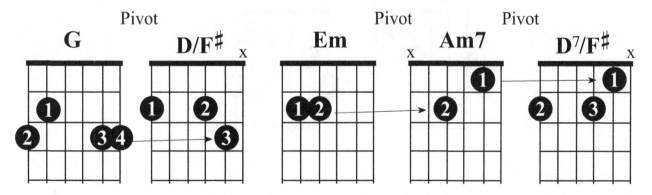

The Chord Changes

In this section, we will focus on the chord changes. The next exercises will prepare us for playing the whole chord progression.

Exercise 47

In this exercise, we will pair up two chords and practice changing back and forth between the two. Practice going back and forth with G to D/F$\sharp$, starting slow and then picking up speed. Do the same with D/F$\sharp$ and Em. Do this same exercise with Em to Am^7, Am^7 to D^7/F$\sharp$, and D^7/F$\sharp$ to G. Pay attention to the pivot and guide fingers.

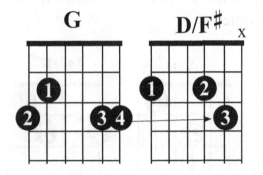

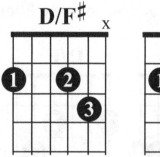

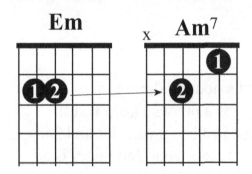

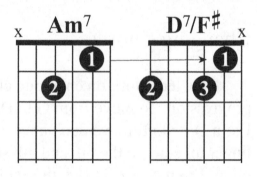

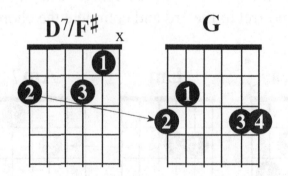

44

The Strum Pattern

The next strum pattern is very important for you to progress on guitar. Practice this pattern using the muted strumming technique we learned earlier in this course. Notice on beat three there is no strum. This is a rest. Do a downstroke on beat three but don't hit any strings so you will stay in motion. There are many strum patterns that involve skipping a downbeat or a downstroke.

Exercise 48

Practice this pattern until can play it easily. This is the most common strum pattern on guitar, so practice it carefully.

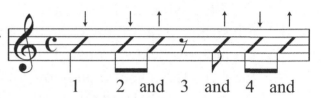

Exercise 49

Now, try the same strum pattern while playing an Em chord.

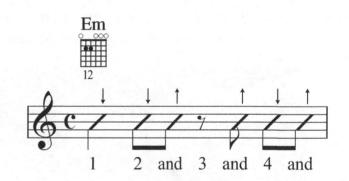

Exercise 50

Practice playing the chord progression along with the strum pattern. Try it slow at first, and then gradually speed it up when you are able.

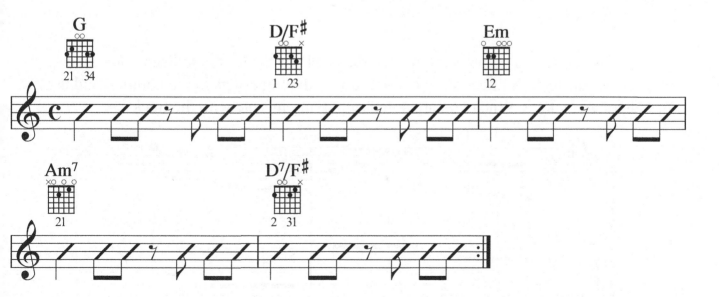

8. New Scales and Exercises

In this section, we are going to work on a few moveable scales. Moveable scales are ones that can played in many places on the guitar neck. To get started, we will first work on a hand position and use it as a stretch and a muscle development technique.

Exercise 51

Place your 1st finger on the 2nd fret 6th string, your 2nd finger on the 3rd fret 6th string, your 3rd finger on the 4th fret, and your pinky on the 5th fret. Examine the pictures below. Notice, I am on the tips of my fingers and toward the front of the frets. Keep your thumb low on the back of the neck and let your wrist drop below the neck. Hold this position in order to get accustomed to it and use it as a stretch and muscle development exercise on a daily basis. This position will enable us to play scales efficiently and accurately. Think of each finger "belonging to a fret".

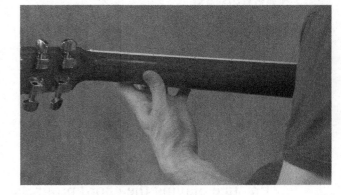

Exercise 52

Using this hand position, practice the G Major Scale. Try to keep your hand spread out so each finger stays in its fret. Use the fingerings in the notation and use alternate picking. When you are able, try playing in time with the track.

46

Exercise 53

Using the same technique, practice the A major scale. This time your first finger will be in the 4th fret and your pinky will be in the 7th fret. We have simply moved our hand up two frets on the guitar. Use alternate picking. When you are able, try playing in time with the track.

Exercise 54

This time we will practice the A minor scale. In order to play this scale, your hand will move up one more fret on the guitar neck, but stay spread out so each finger belongs to a fret. Once again, use alternate picking.

Picking Tips

There are a couple of right hand techniques and positions we should pay attention to when using a pick and playing scales. Your picking hand should be able to move freely and not be anchored in any way on the guitar. It should be similar to strumming the guitar. When you strum, your right hand can move freely up and down. The same should be true when picking single notes or scales. The angle of the pick should be similar on the 1st string to what it is on the 6th string. If our hand moves freely, we will pick each string with essentially the same angle and positioning. If our hand is anchored on the guitar body or saddle, the pick angle for every string will be different. This will cause inconsistencies in playing and tone.

Better

Worse

Better

Worse

9. Bass Notes and a Waltz

In this section, we are going to learn the first of two chord progressions and how to play bass notes along with it. This will also involve playing in 3/4 time or a waltz. Let's start by looking at the chords we will be using and then work on the strum pattern.

Exercise 55

Em and Am we have seen before. The new chord is B^7 and is strummed from the 5th string down. Keep your thumb low on the back of the neck and play towards the front of the frets. Practice each chord on its own and then practice changing chords, making sure to use the pivot fingers.

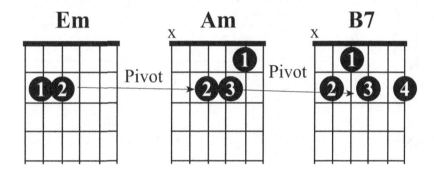

Exercise 56

Let's work on the strum pattern while playing an Em chord. It's all downstrokes but you must play a bass note first. In this case, play the 6th string and then strum from the 4th string down twice. Let the 6th string ring while you strum the others. Since this is in 3/4 time, there will only be three beats to a measure. Count 1,2,3, 1,2,3.

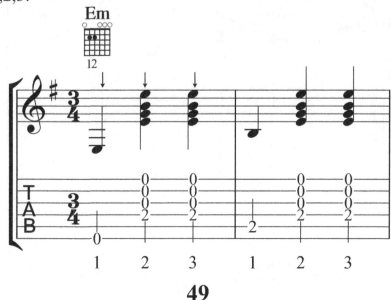

49

Exercise 57

Now, try the strum pattern while playing an Am chord. Again, these are all downstrokes but this time, play the 5th string as the bass note and then strum from the 4th string down, allowing the 5th string to ring.

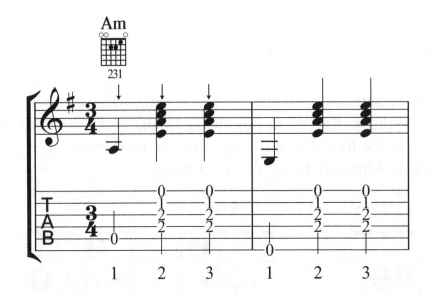

Exercise 58

This time practice the strum pattern while playing a B^7 chord. Use only downstrokes. Play the 5th string as the bass note and then strum from the 4th string down.

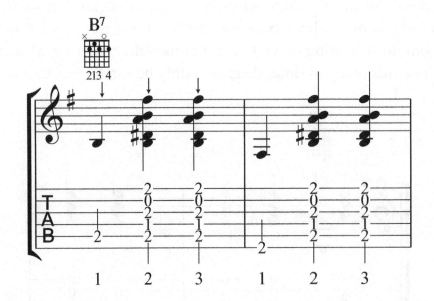

The Chord Progression

Put all of this together and play the whole chord progression. Remember when switching chords to use your pivot fingers. Since this is a waltz, count 1,2,3, 1,2,3.

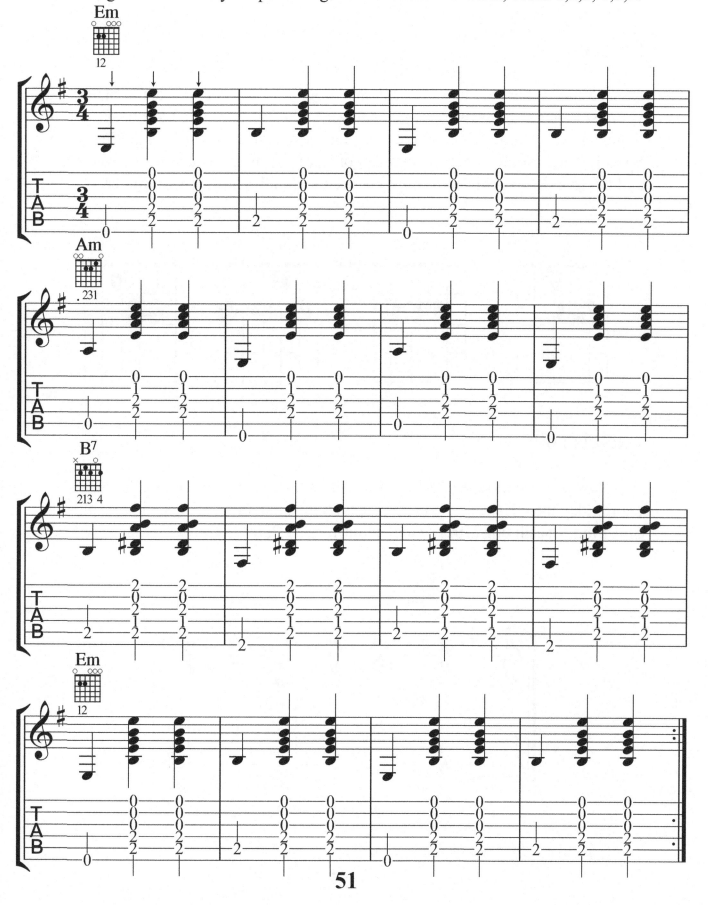

The Chords In E Major

Here are a second set of chords in the key of E major. We'll use these chords to play another waltz. Let's begin by practicing the chords and the chord changes.

Exercise 59

A Major is the only new chord in this progression. It is important to place your 1st finger as far forward as you can get in the 2nd fret. You have to stack your fingers up more vertically to make this chord. Remember to work on getting clean notes for each chord. When changing chords, the 1st finger is a guide between A and B^7. In order to get back to E major, use the 2nd finger as a pivot finger.

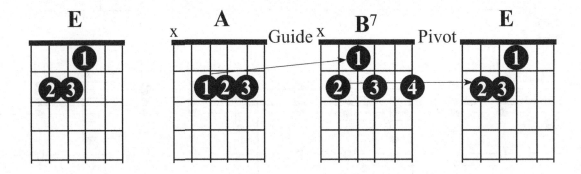

Exercise 60

Now practice the strum pattern we will be using while playing an E major chord. Play the 6th string as your first bass note and then in the second bar, play the 5th string. Use all downstrokes and count 1,2,3, 1,2,3.

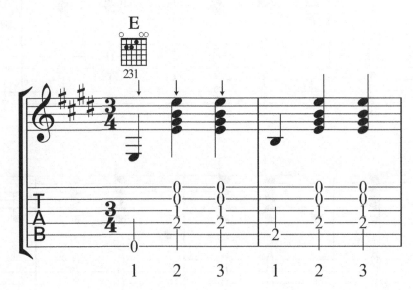

Exercise 61

This time practice the A major chord with the strum pattern. Play the 5th string first and then the 6th string in the 2nd bar.

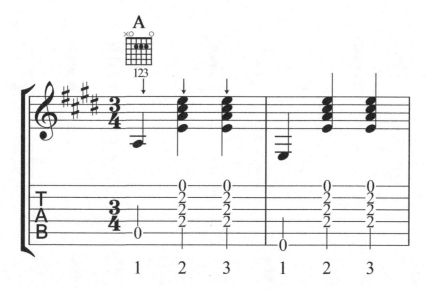

Exercise 62

Once again, we will use the B^7 chord using the same strum pattern as before.

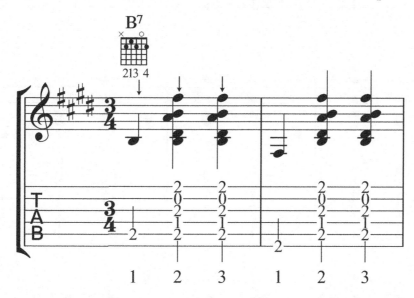

The Chord Progression

What To Do Next

Congratulations! You've just finished Book 1 of our beginner course. Feels good doesn't it? You can review what you've learned so far or start working on Book 2.

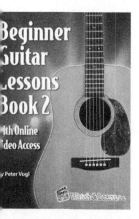

Beginner Guitar Lessons Book 2 with Online Video Access is the follow-up to this course. Learn the tips and tricks that separate a real guitarist from a beginner. Peter will teach you techniques like hammer-ons, pull-offs, and slides along with new chords, progressions, and strumming patterns. Finally, you'll learn how to make basic progressions more exciting by adding embellishments and mixing in riffs with the chords. Using all of the concepts taught in these lessons, you'll be ready to start creating your own music. This course includes over three hours of online HD video instruction.

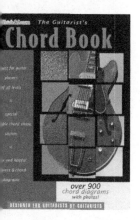

The Guitarist's Chord Book by Peter Vogl is a 144 page book that contains over 900 chords with photos to clearly illustrate each chord and each note of the chord is labeled. It also contains a special moveable chords section with the most widely used shapes for each class of chord. Peter Vogl has also included goodies from his bag of tricks to give you new sounds, shapes, and inspirations for song arrangements. This is a must read for guitar players of all levels .

The Guitarist's Scale Book by Peter Vogl is a complete scale encyclopedia for guitar with over 400 scales and modes. It contains scale diagrams with notation and tablature for each scale and tips on how and when to use each scale. This scale book also contains outside jazz scales, exotic scales, Peter's own Cross-Stringing scales, and easy to understand explanations of scales and modes. This is the only guitar scale book you'll ever need.

These products are available on Amazon.com. If you have any questions, problems, or comments, please contact us at:

Watch & Learn, Inc.
2947 East Point St.
East Point, GA 30344
800-416-7088
sales@cvls.com

Made in the USA
Las Vegas, NV
03 June 2024

90698452R00031